Building

Castles In

The Sky

BUILDING CASTLES IN THE SKY

How To Make Your Dreams Come True

Pamela Sommers

Copyright

Scriptures taken from the Holy Bible, New International Version®, NIV®. Copyright © 1973, 1978, 1984, 2011 by Biblica, Inc.™ Used by permission of Zondervan. All rights reserved worldwide. www.zondervan.com The "NIV" and "New International Version" are trademarks registered in the United States Patent and Trademark Office by Biblica, Inc.™

Edited by Sarah Fox

First Edition

Print ISBN: 978-1-9997391-5-7
Hardcover ISBN: 978-1-9997391-6-4
Epub ISBN: 978-1-9997391-1-9
Mobi ISBN: 978-1-9997391-7-1

I dedicate this book in loving memory of
my mother,

Surya Hurry.

Thank you for your love, kindness,
sense of humour,
and for imparting your wisdom upon
me,
so that I have the courage to build my
own castles in the sky.

I love you always.

CONTENTS

INTRODUCTION

Is there something you've always wanted to do, but, for one reason or another, you haven't got around to doing it? Perhaps you didn't have the courage or were worried about what others would say and how they would react after you had told them about your dreams and goals. Maybe you were worried you would get laughed at or criticised for even thinking your idea was a possibility.

I wrote this book to reassure you that no matter how far-fetched an idea may be to others, their opinions don't make it true, unless you accept it. Many people who have had their original ideas laughed at or dismissed have gone on to become highly successful. Look around you: Everything you touch, even a paperclip, was first thought of as an idea. It was created in someone's imagination first before being made into reality.

'Building castles in the sky' is a metaphor for how you have to create the idea first in your head and imagine it before you are able to make it 'concrete' and turn it into a reality for all to see.

This book is a roadmap for taking your idea out of your head and putting it out into the real world. It will dive deep into the process of turning your dream into reality while guiding you through the steps you need to take regularly. It will involve 'inner' and 'outer' work because you need to be able to change what is within you before you can begin to see and feel the transformation on the outside.

Results begin from within.

This is an exciting time for you!

Are you ready to reach your highest potential and turn your dream into reality?

Great!

Let's begin...

Chapter 1

YOUR THOUGHTS

It's amazing how much of life you take for granted and what you learn from those around you as the truth without exploring it. As children, we tend to follow what our parents or caregivers tell us. When we reach school age, this transfers to learning and retaining information from those around us with influence, such as teachers, priests, and medical staff. For instance, in earlier times, we were taught the times tables by a technique known as 'parrot-fashion', whereby you repeated what the teacher said or read out loud off the board numerous times until you fully grasped the information and hopefully retained it. This method of teaching still goes on in some parts of the world today.

However, in western society, it is somewhat different now. Although children are basically taught by 'parrot-fashion' in the beginning, children are also taught the reason behind an event, how or why a formula is made up, and how a conclusion is reached. This is probably to do with helping the children to understand the process better, whether it is a mathematical equation or a scientific experiment. Children also ask more questions rather than just accepting information. This continues into their adult lives, particularly if they decide to go on to higher education. I remember when I was studying for my A levels. It was somewhat different from the other years. I had to think more and develop more of my own opinions. For instance, in English literature, I was often asked what feelings certain characters evoked and how these emotions were portrayed through their actions and speech. At first, this proved challenging, but after a while, I soon got used to it and actually enjoyed my subjects at a deeper level.

Learning to think for yourself is a big part of growing up. It is easy to let others make decisions for you and give your control to others because then you can blame them and, in a way, let yourself 'off the hook'.

Taking responsibility for your actions is a whole different ball game altogether. It all starts with your thoughts. Being aware of what you think about things has such a big impact on your everyday life. You probably are not aware of it at first. But once you start paying attention to your thoughts, you'll discover that they do affect your actions, whether you realise it or not, these all play a role in shifting your subconscious thought patterns, which are thoughts that lay just beneath the awareness of your mind. They are often brought to the surface while you sleep and may even pop up in your dreams.

To become more aware of and get a better understanding of your regular thought patterns, start off by observing your thoughts. Notice how you react to things or people around you, discover what your opinions are about matters, and find out what triggers certain emotions and responses from you. In other words, explore what really makes you 'tick'. What gets you riled up? Equally, notice what doesn't bother you. Particularly explore what things you remain completely neutral about.

Look for 'clues'; you'll find plenty around you if you look closely enough. It's amazing what hidden depths you'll uncover. You may even find things that surprise yourself and that you are not aware of yet.

For instance, while one driver becomes annoyed at other drivers in traffic and shouts abuse at others, you may find that you are perfectly content to wait for the lights to change colour; perhaps you are enjoying a piece of music on the radio or are happy to be out on a nice, sunny day. In other words, you discover that you have patience and can remain calm while others panic around you.

This is tricky at first because a lot of the time many of us simply say what's on our minds or speak without thinking about what we are saying. The reason it's a good idea to start off by paying attention to our thoughts is that these are what govern our actions.

For example, if you have a bad habit, such as shouting at the television and criticising contestants on a game show, you are far more likely to reduce this response if you go to the root of the problem and find out what started this behaviour in the first place. This way, you have a better chance of resolving any issues or 'nipping things in the bud' before they have a chance to grow.

Tackling the cause, minimises the chances of it being manifested in another way.

For instance, you may have observed your father taking things out on people who are not able to defend themselves and decided if he does it, then it's okay for you to follow suit, especially if your mother didn't say anything to the contrary and simply smiled and went along with your father.

However, if you look around and find that your family hates it when you shout at the television, this should make you think twice and realise that perhaps this isn't such a good habit after all, and you are not doing anyone any favours by acting this way. If you think back to how it all started, it will help you question why you do it and make an effort to stop or at least take control over your

7

reactions. It could be that your father had an issue with failure or that he felt like a 'bigger' man when he shouted or put others down, and this transferred to you growing up, or it could also be that the person on TV getting the question wrong triggered your emotions because you can relate to that, because you feel like you don't know enough or perhaps someone called you 'stupid' once at school.

If you dig deep enough and explore your thoughts, your past, and your emotions, you may be able to do something about it, which can be very empowering and enlightening.

Get quiet and listen. You may be surprised at what you hear. For instance, if you are preparing for something that you feel nervous about, such as a public speaking event or a performance on stage, you may start hearing 'negative' talk. It is also known as the inner critic, which I have mentioned in my previous book, *Life lessons from a 40 something… .* As a reminder, our inner critic stems back from a primitive era whereby it was there to warn us of danger and was a method of safeguarding us. Listen to it, acknowledge what it has to say, and then thank and reassure it by letting it know that you are okay. You could even say to it out loud: 'Thank you, I realise that you are trying to protect me, but I've got this.'

If it helps, search for evidence to confirm things that have recently occurred and how well you handled the situation. These could be in the form of letters of praise from others, thank you cards, great reviews from customers and clients, and compliments from friends. This will also help to reinforce your confidence in your abilities. We are often our own worst critic, so once you have dimmed down your 'negative' thoughts, you can move on.

It may help to write down any observations about any negative thoughts you have, so it is easier to look back on and review.

Miracles happen when we expand and grow mentally, when we are not afraid of reaching higher goals and bigger dreams. This is when we are at our most creative, come up with new ideas, and are generally more upbeat about life and towards those around us.

Try keeping a journal of your thoughts for a week. If it helps, set a regular time every day to jot down your thoughts and observations. By the end of the week, you will probably start noticing a pattern emerging. You can get excited because this means you actually are doing something about it. Once you see patterns of your thoughts emerging, you can go through them one by one.

For instance, if you worry that you do not know enough or that you are not good enough in a particular subject, you can learn and study it a little more and then apply the knowledge. This will then help you feel more confident about it and remove this obstacle from your thoughts. When you go through the obstacles one step at a time, they will free up your headspace, so you can replace them with more positive thoughts to help you feel good about yourself.

Chapter 2

YOUR WORDS

Your words are more powerful than you realise. They can be used to encourage and build someone up, or they can be destructive. How you choose to use your words can play an important role in how you make others around you feel. It's up to you how you decide to use and how you choose your words.

If you choose to use your words in a negative way, they can torture a soul more than you'll ever know. I'm sure you can recall many negative words or phrases that 'haunt' you. It may have been an argument with your spouse or best friend, whereby both parties said some harsh words in the heat of the moment. Whatever the case and whenever this has happened, both parties more often than not usually feel horrible afterwards and may be filled with regrets. It makes no difference. Once words have been said, they can never be taken back, even if they are said out of anger. So, choose your words wisely.

On the other hand, words can envelop and comfort a troubled soul, lift someone up if he or she is feeling down, and brighten up the day. For instance, if you are walking down the road and someone greets you in a friendly way and wishes you a pleasant day, you automatically feel good about yourself and those around you.

There are many times when people say what they think. Unfortunately, this isn't always a good thing, especially if there is alcohol involved, because you never know which way it will turn out. I'm sure you have heard the saying: 'think before you speak'. Well, for the majority of the time, this is a good idea. For instance, you may be attending a special occasion, and someone may just make a little comment about how you look without thinking. If the words are said in the wrong way or at the wrong time, everything could become blown out of proportion and escalate unnecessarily.

Of course, it isn't always just the words themselves that matter, but the way you say things (i.e. the tone of your voice and your body language) can affect others' reactions too. For example, a couple has had an argument. The man asks his spouse how she is feeling, and she replies, 'I'm fine' in an abrupt manner. She has her arms folded and looks away while she is speaking. It is generally implied that she clearly is not fine at all, despite what she says.

Words have often been linked to reputation. For instance, historically, when a person said, 'I give you my word', It was almost like a verbal contract, and the parties involved seldom had reason to doubt one another. Reputation was perceived by how you presented yourself, and your words played an integral part in this. It was traditionally associated with trust and honesty. In a nutshell, words carried merit and were rarely said in haste.

However, over time, things have changed, and a person can no longer take words at face value. Rather than taking a person's word as gospel, as was done in the past, contracts have to be made in writing, making it formal. This is to protect against the off chance that someone is not as sincere as he or she appears and also to protect both parties involved. As, unfortunately, trust is not always well-placed.

Developing a positive mindset can help when interacting with others as well as yourself. A good habit to try is to listen out for any self-talk or advice you give yourself. For instance, if you drop something on the floor, do you mentally scold yourself or do you just pick the object up and carry on? This type of talk can give clues as to how you feel about yourself and how you have learned certain behaviour and opinions from your parents or other authority figures. If you do speak badly toward yourself, make a note of it, as this could be something to work on at a deeper level.

It is also worth paying attention to how you react to others around you too. For instance, if you hear a nasty comment, what do you tell yourself in your head? Do you immediately get defensive and go on the attack? Do you think that you know better and rebel by doing the opposite of what they expect or want? Or do you humour them and remain calm and composed and continue with your day? These signs can be very telling.

Listen for the good things you tell yourself too because we want to encourage these. When you focus on the 'positive' self-talk, you will start to see yourself in a better light and have a more expansive energy about you. In other words, you feel as though you can achieve anything you put your mind to, which enables you to grow to your full potential.

There are a variety of methods to use to help improve your self-talk and how you view yourself.

Hypnotherapy is a great method used by practitioners to delve into your subconscious and help uncover hidden beliefs around why you do or act in certain ways. For example, if you are afraid of flying, perhaps you had a bad flying experience as a child. Hypnotherapy can put you in a deep state of relaxation and unravel your beliefs and thoughts around your fear and confirm why there is no reason to be so fearful. This way, you feel like you are able to conquer the fear.

EFT, otherwise known as Emotional Freedom Technique or

'tapping', is a method whereby you tap on meridian points; these are a network of channels that transport energy to certain points of the body. This method has often been found to help relieve and release the stress or anxiety around a specific problem. Alternatively, talking to someone about the problem can feel like a huge weight has been lifted off your shoulders.

You may find that it all starts from an early memory, possibly from childhood. Once you know when or why it started, you can analyse it and focus on shifting the problem at a deeper level in your subconscious.

Be prepared, this can be quite an emotional experience, but it can bring about quite a transformation in your mindset, your energy, and how you feel about yourself. You start feeling that you can accomplish anything you put your mind to.

Here's a useful exercise to try, which can help you discover more about your self-talk and the impact it can have:

Get yourself a notepad or journal and jot down what type of phrases naturally pops in your head throughout the day. Do this a few times a day and perhaps in the evening before you go to bed. Don't judge yourself; just write them down. After a week, have a read through them. You may find a few surprises. That's okay.

The next stage is to go through the 'negative' or discouraging ones and ask yourself why you tell yourself that. Is it a habit? Then try to recall when you first started doing this. It could stem back from an early childhood memory. This way, you get to the root of the reason and can do something about it. If it was from something painful at the time (i.e. being laughed at on stage), consider the relevance of that situation now and how it fits in with your adult self.

More often than not, you will discover that the negative belief you have about this situation is no longer relevant. If that is the case, which is usually what most people find, take a deep breathe in and imagine yourself breathing the negative belief out. This is a method of releasing these beliefs so that you can make space for much more positive beliefs. Do this slowly. It may take some time, and you may need to do this a few times, but that's fine because it will help you in the long run.

Eventually you will start to feel better about the situation. If,

however, you find there is still
some of the old, unwanted beliefs
remaining, it may help to consult
a professional to help you, such
as an EFT practitioner or
hypnotherapist. These experts are
trained and are used to helping
people resolve these
circumstances. Now that you have
found the root of the problem,
you are able to do something
about it, and this alone can be
very empowering.

Return to this exercise
whenever you feel you need to.
And before you know it, you will
be able to manage 'negative' talk.

Now let's look at the
'positive' self-talk, which can be
identified as giving yourself
words of encouragement. In the
same way as the previous
exercise, go through your list, ask
yourself why you said this, and
notice how it made you feel about

yourself. If you can, try to remember back to when you first had these good feelings.

Whenever you feel happy and find yourself in a wonderful state of mind and want this moment to last forever, try this helpful technique to remind yourself of a time when you were completely happy: Place your thumb and middle finger or forefinger together while you are thinking of that happy time and having these feelings. This is known as 'anchoring'. When you anchor these feelings, you remember the positive experiences. Do this for a few seconds. Whenever you are feeling down or 'out of sorts', if you touch the same fingers together, it reminds you of the 'anchored' positive experiences you have had in the past and acts as a reminder that 'life is good' and that you can achieve what you set out to. This way, you can carry these positive moments around with you wherever you go.

Now that we've gotten to the bottom of your self-talk, observe how you speak to others and the words you say. Likewise, listen to conversations around you and what others say to you. You will soon start noticing the positive influences and the opposite. This also applies to television, radio, and other media around you.

For instance, soap operas rely on drama and unhappy events to gain viewers' attention, so that they want to know what happens next, which is almost always a negative storyline.

On the other hand, hearing about someone winning the lottery and being reunited with a relative on the other side of the world on the radio, is an example of something positive. Once you start noticing these, it isn't unusual to find yourself leaning towards the more positive influences and begin moving away from the not-so-positive ones. This is a good thing and is a sign that you are growing and moving forward.

Chapter 3

YOUR ACTIONS

How you think about yourself and others is naturally expressed in your words and through your body language. How you speak to yourself in your mind—in other words, self-talk is just as important as how you talk to others. For instance, if you are about to do something you have never done before, try listening to your inner voice. What is it telling you? Can you hear words of encouragement or does it scold you for trying and attempts to dissuade you? You can often tell if people listen to positive self-talk by their posture and how they carry themselves; they appear more confident and walk tall, ready to embrace life. On the other hand, people who often listen to their negative self-talk tend to look the opposite; they may slouch or look down when they speak and give the impression that they do not value themselves as much.

Your internal dialogue has a significant impact on how you view yourself. It can affect your confidence, your mood, and even how you walk. For instance, when you see someone stand with their head raised, looking interested and facing forward; the likelihood is that the person is mentally listening to encouraging words. On the other hand, if you see someone looking down with slouched shoulders, the chances are that person is hearing negative things. Perhaps the person is even putting himself or herself down, before the activity has even begun. This in itself can be a self-fulfilling prophecy as by thinking in a defeatist manner, one is more likely to have an unsuccessful outcome.

You've no doubt heard the phrase: 'Actions speak louder than words.' This also applies to your mindset. The actions you take almost always reflect how you think and feel about yourself.

Body language plays an integral role in this. How you carry and hold yourself 'speaks' volumes without you even having to utter a word.

By walking tall you will have an air of confidence about you, which people will realise as soon as they see you. First impressions count. If you are perceived to be confident, those around you will instantly feel reassured and believe that you are in control. This also makes it easier for them to trust you, especially if you speak in a clear and firm tone.

If, on the other hand, you are walking with uncertain footsteps and fidgeting nervously, this sends out the message that you are unsure of yourself, which is more likely to result in people not willing to put their faith in you. Your speech may also be affected as you may start stuttering or speaking quietly, which could also signify that you lack confidence.

Posture is very telling. Try it for yourself. See how you feel and check your thoughts about yourself. Sit down on your sofa and observe how you sit. If you are slouched and lean forward towards the edge of your seat, chances are you feel slightly on edge. If you sit back and your feet are firmly on the ground, this shows that you are at ease with yourself and those around you. If you love to lie on the couch, well, I think you know what that means; what other people think doesn't bother you, and you adore your creature comforts. Obviously, how you sit on your sofa at home may be very different from how you sit on a sofa if you are visiting someone.

Start noticing your posture and your body language in everyday life. Try this for a week, and I bet you can pick up on a few things. You may have habits that you never even realised you had. Jot these down.

This will inevitably lead you to start noticing the body language and actions of others around you. In fact, you may even catch yourself trying to correct them because you realise the effects it can have on their overall image, but you don't want to do this too often because you don't want to alienate others.

Of course, you don't just have to stick to situations in your life to observe this. If you have particular celebrities you admire, observe how they carry themselves and listen to how they speak. Actors and actresses put a lot of effort into their deportment and speech. This is all part of how they get into character.

Watching and acting like people you admire is a good, old-fashioned confidence trick. If you are not feeling confident, you may want to try this out:

Take a look in the mirror and say a certain phrase. It could be something like: 'You are gorgeous.' At first, you may feel a little silly and may act a little coy.

Now imagine you have stepped into the shoes of someone famous you admire. Say it again: 'You are gorgeous.' Get into character and have fun with it. No one is watching you, so you can continue this role play. Now say it like you mean it. Say it like the person you admire would say it.

Observe your posture, your expression, and the sound of your voice. Above all, how does it make you feel?

I expect you feel like you can conquer the world, right? This feeling is like gold dust, but the magic and the beauty of it is that you can have this feeling over and over again whenever you want to.

One suggestion is to physically imagine the gold dust in your hand and place it in your heart to tap into whenever you wish. This way, whenever you feel like you are not brave enough, you can tap into this feeling, which acts as a reminder that you can do it. If that is too much for you, do what's right for you. You could even 'anchor' this feeling like I mentioned in the previous chapter (you put your thumb and fingers together and remember a happy time). Practise this as many times as you want and do what feels comfortable for you. This will help you feel great about yourself and can be uplifting.

You can create your own 'feel good' techniques to help you feel comfortable with yourself. When you start putting these into place, others around you will soon start noticing a difference in you, even though they won't be able to put their fingers on it at first.

Body language is just one form of taking action. Taking action is a process made up of a number of consistent steps. First and foremost, it all starts with making the decision to go for it, even before putting things in motion. This takes mental preparation in the form of effort, passion, drive, and determination before even embarking on the practical steps.

It may help to write down the steps you need to do in order to achieve your required outcome. The steps involved could be as simple as researching a prospective client, sending an email, or even picking up the phone. Action is always required to move on to the next level. Sometimes it may seem uncomfortable because you are doing something you wouldn't usually do, but, like most things, the more often you do it, the easier it becomes until it feels like it's almost second nature.

For instance, if you have a public speaking event coming up, do as much preparation as you can. Write down the main points you want to address and perhaps think of stories to tell related to the topic or use a couple of examples to help guide you through delivering your message. Rehearse what you want to say in front of a mirror or even practice in front of a family member or friend. Then if you still feel anxious or nervous about going on stage, a good tip to remember is to think how would [insert name of someone you admire, such as a personal hero or celebrity] do it? What would he or she say? How would that person handle this situation? This can help soothe your nerves and transform you into a person of strength. In a way, you are 'borrowing' this strength from your imaginary friend, but guess what?

The strength lies within you. For you are in control; it is your imagination and your body. Now there's a surprise, huh? You are doing it all. You are in charge, and it is your show. If you are going to act a part, it may as well be the lead role.

What are you waiting for? I believe in you. You totally own this!

After you have observed and practised these methods, it will soon seem like second nature to you. This is a fantastic achievement and will have a greater impact than you realise. Who knows? You may also inspire those around you to greatness.

Chapter 4

VISUALISE

Every success story began with an idea, whether it started from a moment of inspiration or a dream. Athletes, business people, actors, experts, and other successful people all have this in common. Without the first thought or concept, many of these ideas would have never made their way into reality.

To keep this dream alive, it takes a lot of perseverance and discipline as well as hard work. However, keeping an idea alive doesn't just require practical elements like hard work and strategies. You need to start from within to establish and obtain the best results. Our mind is indeed a remarkable gift and can even be used as a tool or instrument to help us achieve and fulfil our wildest dreams or desires. Of course, this takes training and practice. It doesn't just happen overnight. Just as the body needs to practice and train to succeed in a marathon or fitness regime, so does our mind in order to achieve what we have set out to do.

Training your mind to be quiet, calm, and still can take a lot of discipline, patience, and practice. There are various methods to help you reach your desired goal. Meditation can be one way to achieve this. You can sit quietly for periods of time and listen to a piece of music or guided meditation. Some even like to chant, but you don't have to. You could just sit in silence and notice what comes up in your mind. Prayer is also another method of placing yourself in a calm state, which can help as you focus on God and gratitude. Another form is visualisation.

When you regularly visualise or focus on an outcome, you are focusing your energy and your entire being on an idea you'd like to see come to fruition. The activity is not as important as the habit itself. Giving focus to any activity on a regular basis enables energy to flow to it and strengthen it, thus increasing your chance of success.

If you have never experienced this before, don't worry; it's not as hard as you may think. There are many guided visualisations available on the internet, and these will help you. You may

41

wish to do this to music in the background or in silence, whichever you prefer. Here is a brief overview of what's involved:

- Find somewhere where you won't be disturbed and either sit up straight or lie down.
- Close your eyes.
- Take a deep breath and inhale for a count of five.
- Slowly exhale to release tension.
- Repeat this method of breathing a couple of times.
- Imagine slowly walking down the stairs and count backwards from ten on each step you walk down.
- When you reach the bottom of the stairs, imagine walking out through some double doors into a beautiful garden.

- You find a bench. Go and sit there. It is a gorgeous, sunny day, and you can see an array of colourful flowers, and the grass is so vibrantly green.
- You can hear the birds singing, and you can feel the gentle warmth on your skin.
- All is well.
- Now imagine your ideal self in your ideal day.
- Notice all the details. What are you wearing? Who are you with? What sounds can you hear? What activities are you doing? Most of all, how do you feel?
- Absorb how you feel and the effect you have on others. Notice the happiness you bring to others and bask in this feeling of deep joy and deep love for a few minutes.

- Now slowly rise from the bench and walk through the beautiful garden, taking in the fresh summer air and continue listening to the birds singing.
- Start walking up the stairs slowly while counting up to ten with each step.
- Now, begin re-connecting to your familiar surroundings. Start by moving your feet, your hands, your neck, and shoulders. Breath in and out slowly twice before gradually opening your eyes.
- All is still well in the world.

Doing this visualisation regularly, even if it's only once a week (although ideally ten minutes a day), will help you feel at ease with yourself. It will give you a sense of calm with the reassurance that your goal is achievable. It can be done. You have seen it in your mind and felt it. This makes it all the more real because even though others can't see it yet, even though it seems so far off in the distant future, it doesn't mean it won't happen. It doesn't make it any less real. You have to think of it first before you can move forward. You have to be able to imagine it happening before it actually happens. Above all, you have to 'feel' that it is real, so you can see it through to the end. Really act as if it is happening right now; relay to yourself what you can hear, taste, and smell. What clothes are you wearing? Who are you with? This will accelerate the pace of turning it into reality.

Basically, you have to 'build castles in the sky' before you can build them on the ground. Even

in the days of the Bible and other
historical times, many ideas
started from dreams that
occurred. This seemed perfectly
natural back then, but somehow
this concept has been forgotten.
Having said that, many artists
still get moments of inspiration
while they are in a dream-like
state. This can occur for writers,
musicians, actors, and many
more. I for one can confirm this
from experience because, as I
mentioned in *Life Lessons from a
40 Something*... I sleep with a
notepad next to my bed so I can
jot my ideas down.

However, you want to refer to
it—daydreaming, ideas, or
visions—it is a part of the process
of reaching, achieving, and
accomplishing your goals. They
are like the seeds of success,
which if cared for and nurtured,
will sprout up and thrive.

Be filled with gratitude when you get these creative ideas. See them as moments of opportunity to flourish and inspire those around you. Encourage others to also believe and tune into their dreams. For you never know where your imagination will take you.

Chapter 5

ALL GOOD THINGS

Gratitude is a part of the process of achieving what you want out of life and reaching your goals. For the more you are grateful for, the more you attract similar things to be grateful for into your life. This is because you are creating positive energy, which is expansive.

Your happier feelings will have an impact on all people and things around you. When you feel good, you attract positive situations and things to you. In basic terms, you attract 'like for like'. This positive feeling is energy. We can't see it or touch it, but we can somehow feel it. When you are in a happy environment, you can sense the positivity around you. This is also referred to as a 'high vibration', which can occur when you are in a positive frame of mind and everything runs smoothly and falls into place. It is when you feel very happy. High vibes generally speed up the metabolism and create a feeling of enthusiasm and excitement in you and can also influence those around you.

In other words, you are leading by example. If someone sees how vibrant and full of energy you are, they become curious and may ask you: 'How come you are so full of beans?' and 'Can you share any advice?' This is what creates momentum. Once there is momentum in something you want to accomplish, such as growing your business or completing a task, things start happening. You start seeing results and achieving goals. People start acknowledging you, and this all helps propel you to success.

Naturally, you want this feeling to last as long as possible and enjoy this experience. Be prepared, this may require a lot of energy, so try and remain grounded.

When you are in this high-vibe frequency, everything goes your way or at least the way it should.

While you are in this happy state, it is important to take a moment to express gratitude. Look around you and take in all the good things that are in your life. This could include your family, your friends, your home, garden, car, and whatever you are grateful for. Take a deep breath, absorb this feeling, and then let the air out slowly. You deserve to lap up all these happy moments.

If you don't already, make it a habit to think of things you are grateful for every day. You could say it out loud in the morning or before you go to sleep. You can even set a reminder during the day. That way, if your day isn't going so great, this could help change your mood and place you in a happier disposition.

If you meet someone who complains about life or what isn't going well, encourage him or her to look at what is going right and try and steer the conversation towards the good things that are happening. Sometimes it isn't always easy to see what you have until someone else mentions it. Everyone has a different point of view, and what one person observes another may have missed. You never know, this could brighten up that person's whole outlook, not only during that particular day, but in life as a whole.

It's easy to look at the things that aren't going right. Sometimes it can be a challenge to think of the good things, but with a whole lot of practice and a little persuasion, it can be done. If you don't try, you'll never know. We all have to start somewhere and at some point, so it may as well be now.

Make a list of all the things that you are grateful for. At first, you may find it hard, but be patient with yourself and give yourself time to get into this. See it like a game. Start by naming three things you are grateful for and then increase it to five, then seven, then ten, and so forth.

Before you know it, you'll be so busy counting your blessings that you won't have time to even think about the bad stuff, let alone talk about it.

Once you get the hang of this new habit, it will come as second nature to you. You'll find you get to a point where you no longer require prompting and do it automatically. This is great as long as you remember to have a feeling behind it, such as passion and purpose. It's the feeling and intent behind the word that create the impact. Otherwise, they are just words, and you may as well be reciting a shopping list. Feelings that support your words are what count.

You should also start noticing a change in your mood and your temperament, and you may find yourself stopping to smile at yourself, as you begin to feel truly grateful for all you have. For instance, when you sit out in the garden, you may find yourself listening to the birds sing while you enjoy the scenery. You may even relax into a state of bliss and get into a meditative state, where you feel calm and at peace with your surroundings and all that is. You may have heard someone before mention about 'being at one with nature'. You will finally understand what that person means.

It is inevitable that others will soon start noticing the change in you. Share this method of being grateful with them. The more people know about this, the more they will also practise gratitude, and this can only bring good into the world, and that is always positive.

So, take a moment right now and pause whatever you are

doing. Think or say out loud three things you are grateful for right now. Don't think too long about it; just say whatever comes to mind.

Then notice how you feel. Does it bring a smile to your face? Does it make you feel calm? Did you find it hard at first or was it easier than you thought it was going to be?

You may find yourself feeling a little more relaxed and at ease with yourself. This is because you have reminded yourself of what is going great for you, which can give a sense of reassurance and peace. Sometimes it is just an inner knowing that all is well in the world and nothing is ever as bad as you think it is. You may also be surprised to discover the number of things that are actually going well in your life. You have

many, many blessings. Start
counting them with gratitude.

Chapter 6

STAYING GROUNDED

When you have grasped and felt
the momentum rising within you,
it will make you want to take
action and move faster. At this
point, it is so easy to get carried
away or become distracted by the
latest shiny object or other ideas.
Everything can be so exciting at
first and getting caught up in
what others are doing is all too
easy. Try not to get swept away
by those around you. They may
not understand what you are
trying to accomplish. This can
take away from you focusing on
the task at hand. For example,
you may be in the middle of

writing an email, and your spouse may ask you to look at something funny on TV. To avoid situations like these, it is a good idea to say that you need to concentrate on something right now, and after you have finished, take a break and spend some time with him or her.

We are only human, and while it is quite natural to stop and look at what our friends are doing, curiosity can also have a negative impact on ourselves. Remember what happened to the cat?

Instead, try to conserve your energy and focus on your own intentions. This will help you keep to the matter at hand so that you don't lose sight of what you are trying to achieve.

Staying grounded—which means being stable, balanced, and strong—is a way of keeping you humble and for you to realise that you are part of a bigger picture. You have been given your gift for a reason, whether it's offering support to others, having a valuable product to share, or creating ideas that will inspire a generation. What you do is all part of the process. You are necessary. You matter.

When you remain true to yourself, you are indirectly showing yourself and others respect: respect for your gift, respect for human nature, and respect for others. By allowing others to see the real you, even if that means being vulnerable at times, you give them a chance to get to know you. This creates an appreciation for yourself and honesty. It also makes you easier to relate to.

We all require energy, and when you see a creative task into fruition, a lot of energy is needed.

You don't want to feel as though you are finished before you have started. You need your energy to maintain the momentum that is needed to succeed in what you do. This goes for physical as well as mental energy.

There are a number of disciplines you can try to help with this.

With regards to mental energy, you could meditate or pray regularly. The art of being still and quiet creates a somewhat holy experience. It helps us realise where we are and who we are in the grander scheme of things.

Physical energy can also be kept under control, especially if you are feeling as though your head is all over the place and you are trying to do lots of things at the same time, but you are getting nowhere.

Try this exercise to help you stay grounded.

- Stand upright with your arms spread out in the shape of a tree.
- Close your eyes and imagine the roots of a tree flowing down both legs and through both of your feet.
- Now imagine the roots going deeper and deeper into the grass and soil and deeper still into the earth beneath.
- Stay completely aligned with your body and hold for a count of five or longer.
- You should be feeling strong and standing firm. Your foundations should feel so strong that they cannot be moved.
- Now slowly open your eyes. Move your arms back down beside you and take a

couple of deep breaths in and out.

- You will now feel poised and have a calming stillness about you.

This exercise has helped me numerous times in my life. It's so easy to become swept away with all the business that is going on around us.

There are times where we just have to stop, go somewhere quiet, and breathe. Breathing itself can be soothing; It all depends on the technique. For example. If you breathe too fast, it can have the opposite effect and create a sense of panic, whereas if you take your time, slow down the pace a little, and breath in and out slowly, it can have a calming and therapeutic effect. You are no longer fighting for attention from different parts of your mind and body; you are functioning together as one unit and one purpose. Your body, mind, and spirit are all working in unison to keep you grounded and prepared for action and for success. And because you are strong and healthy, this places you in a better position to help others along their path. For they will see that you live by example, and, therefore, they are more likely to listen to what you have to say. Everything is congruent.

Staying grounded and full of grace is a necessary skill that has to be practised. Patience and perseverance go hand in hand, and very few things happen overnight. Be patient with yourself. There will be times when no matter how hard you try, you can't stay still. Perhaps you should be flexible at that time and wait for another day before trying again. Don't let that put you off.

Try again until you develop your own method.

Of course, this is just one method of becoming grounded. If it doesn't work for you, try something else; perhaps you are more suited to gardening, walking in nature, sewing, drawing, or even doing something much more physical, such as dancing or exercising. As long as you take a break from your thoughts for at least a few minutes, you will feel better. It could also throw some light on a matter that was troubling you before. Just think, by trying something completely different, you will be gaining a whole new perspective, and who knows? This could work out for the better.

Try to practise some form of grounding exercise regularly. This will help to keep you going on a daily basis. You are more

likely to continue when you stop
for regular breaks as opposed to
running full steam ahead without
taking time out. Consider the
bigger picture in all you do.

Chapter 7

INNER GUIDANCE

Guidance is something we all need from time to time, particularly if we are going through a transition phase in life like leaving for college or leaving home for the first time. Of course, it is good to ask for guidance on matters you know nothing or very little about before you decide to go ahead with a plan. However, there are times when we have to stop looking to others for answers to our question.

Some people ask others incessantly. At times, it could be because they don't know or because they become lazy and it is easier to ask others rather than take the time to find out for themselves.

It can also be a sign that they lack confidence in their own abilities to make decisions and may not even trust their own judgement.

If this is the case for you, it's time to nip this in the bud as soon as possible before it becomes a habit. While it's often nice to obtain the opinion of others, self-reliance can be a beautiful thing.

Before you move forward, it may be a good idea to sit down and take a moment to ask yourself why you feel the need to rely on others' opinion or advice instead of trusting yourself. Do you doubt yourself? If so, what has happened in the past to make this so? It may take some time to discover these answers, but once you have an idea of what is keeping you from making a judgement call, you are able to do something about it. Only you will know the real answer. No one knows you like you do. Indeed, you may hire a coach or mentor to try and coax it out of you, but he or she still won't know you inside out. Even your best friend, mother, or sibling won't have all the answers. Sometimes you just have to bite the bullet and do things on your own. As scary as this sounds, once you have done this, it will become easier, and you will soon gain the confidence to trust in your own judgement and follow your inner guidance.

Once you have found out why you doubt yourself, you may find it has something to do with your childhood memories or something else that occurred in the past. If this is the case, try and go through the event as you recall it one stage at a time. Try and recapture the details and feelings you had around the event; write these down in a journal. Chances are you will have a whole new stance on what happened after you have looked back on it. Oftentimes, when doing this exercise, you may realise that things weren't as bad as you first thought. You could also discover how things may have been blown out of proportion or understand the reasons behind a particular scenario. For instance, if your parents were harsh with you, it could be that they were under a lot of pressure at the time and took it out on whoever was around.

Play this memory back in your head, and now look at it as the person you are now. Observe how you feel and what you can learn from this. For instance, looking back, you may now realise that your parents didn't mean anything personally, and it doesn't mean that you are to blame for that situation. Although this exercise can be painful, it will help you move forward in a big way. Once you face your triggers head on, it places you in a position of strength. You now have the power to shift this mental obstacle and clear the path for bigger and brighter things to come.

Now you can begin to move forward. When you are searching for guidance, get quiet and make sure you are relaxed. Close your eyes if it helps, ask your inner guidance the questions you have, trust that you have been heard, and then above all listen. This may sound obvious, but it's surprising the number of times we expect answers right away, but we do not take the time to wait for them or even listen.

Simply stay quiet for a little while and wait for a response of some form. You may just receive an inner knowing or it may be a feeling that you get. If it's a decision that you are making, observe how you feel. You may feel at calm or at peace when you lean towards one decision and feel uneasy about the other option. If this is the case, go with the one you feel at ease with.

You may not receive the answer immediately. Don't worry; it always arrives at just the right time. Go and do something else completely different, and the answer will come to you when you are ready to receive it. This could be later in the day, during the week, or while you are asleep. You will receive it as long as you let go and don't try to control it.

Instead, trust your inner guidance.

This doesn't mean you don't have to weigh the pros and cons of a situation. You can still write it down on paper if it helps you. Just don't overthink it and make yourself more confused.

Clarity is what is required here, so learn to take a step back, take a deep breath, and go within.

When you have done this a few times, it can feel very liberating and empowering because not everyone is always around to ask things. Sometimes you just have to figure things out yourself, even if you don't want to. While it's good to ask others for advice at the beginning or now and then, you'll soon discover that it is far more enriching to learn to trust your inner guidance. We all have this gift; it may come through as a voice making suggestions or as a feeling or an inner knowing of what is right. As with most things, the more you practice this skill, the easier it will become until you get to the point where you instantly do it without realising. Don't be a drifter and look to others for answers all the time; stand firm and trust your inner guidance.

Chapter 8

IT'S YOUR CHOICE

Surround yourself with positivity, whether this is with your friends, family, acquaintances, or people you meet. Everyone needs a starting point, and your closest circle is naturally a good place to begin.

You may not realise it, but those around you have a great deal of influence on you. Since you were born, you have been influenced. First by your parents or caregivers, then by authority figures (such as teachers and their assistants), and then by your friends and colleagues. Some of these people have been chosen by you, and many haven't. While it is true that you cannot control everything or everyone, you can do something about your choice. So focus on what you can do and on your freedom of choice.

We make choices every day: what we eat, what we wear, what books we read, and what programmes we watch on TV. Not all the decisions we make are good ones. This is part of life and how we learn about ourselves and those around us. Some people are better at making decisions than others. For instance, leaders—such as politicians, business owners, and managers are always making decisions and tend to make more decisions than others. While, they may not always make the right decisions, their overall experience in decision-making equips them to make more successful choices.

Therefore, the more chances you have to make decisions, the better you will become at making them, and the more likely you are to succeed.

These decisions are not just limited to the boardroom or work matters. Personal choices also have a great effect on our lives. When you choose a friend, they can either have a negative or positive impact on you. For instance, if you are in school or college, troublesome friends, who are often associated with lots of drama, may seem exciting and lots of fun to be around initially, but after a while, the things they do may begin to affect you academically, especially if you start to try and please them to retain their friendships or to look 'cool' in front of them. It may only be a gradual change, which you hardly notice at first. It is

79

always best to realise this before it is too late. It is better to do something about it while you still can by minimising the time spent in their company and focusing on what's important to you and your personal goals. Otherwise, this may affect you later in life.

When it's someone you can choose, such as a friend, it is manageable, but what if you are related to someone? This can be quite tough as there is no getting away from the fact that sooner or later you have to be in the same room. If it is an aunt or uncle or a distant relative that you don't see very often, it is best to offer 'pleasantries' with a smile and understand that in the scheme of things, you are only with them for a short length of time. Once you place some perspective on the matter, it may not seem quite as daunting. This isn't always easy, especially when the other person makes nasty or spiteful remarks. It's human nature to want to bite back with a nasty comment in return. Sometimes the best way is to say something nice back, albeit through gritted teeth. That way you will throw the person off-guard, and it would be completely unexpected as he or she will be expecting a mean remark back. Surprise often has a way of working its magic.

Try and minimise the time you spend with someone negative as much as you can. This way, his or her habits won't rub off on you. This is easier said than done, but if you at least try, you'll be doing yourself a favour. Aim to feel good about yourself as much as possible by doing more of the things that bring you joy and focus on your own positive qualities. For example, spend time on things you are good at, such as playing an instrument or a particular sport. This way, you will soon realise who uplifts you and who tries to do the opposite. You deserve to feel your best and to keep a positive frame of mind.

Don't feel guilty about feeling happy and enjoying your life. We are all here for such a short time so we may as well make the most of it. As long as you are not hurting anyone else, what's the harm?

Once you have got this under control, you can start applying this to other areas of your life. For instance, as I mentioned in Chapter 2: Observe how you feel after you watch certain programmes on TV. Ask yourself: How do I feel after I watch a soap opera? Does it uplift or entertain me or do I feel drained and emotional? After you have done this a few times, you may start to notice a pattern. This is when you can choose to do something about it. I say 'choose' because you are in control of this. It doesn't have to be a case of just watching a programme out of habit. You decide what information to retain in your brain and what visual imagery to see or to avoid. Don't let others decide for you. The media is only too happy to influence you if you let it.

The same goes for the books, magazines, or newspapers you read; the radio stations you listen to; the places you go to; and, of course, the company you keep. Find out for yourself by selecting media that bring you joy and keep you in a positive frame of mind. Once you start feeling the difference these make, you will be encouraged to continue in your mission to feel happy as much as you can, which will have a positive impact on those around you.

It is all too easy to just 'let' things happen to you and accept things as they are. By doing this, you are giving your power away. The power of choice is in your hands. You can decide to follow or take the lead and feel empowered by making your own decisions. Which will you choose?

Chapter 9

YOUR DREAMS

In Biblical times and throughout history, dreams have often been profound. They were usually thought of as a way of delivering messages to inspire action from the person dreaming. For example, Joseph received a message about Jesus being the Son of God in a dream. Today, dreams are often dismissed as being part of the subconscious; however, they sometimes have an uncanny way of getting to the heart of a problem by offering a solution.

As we go through the days, our subconscious collects and

stores information. Some of this may seem trivial, and we hardly notice them while, at other times, they can seem more significant. Nevertheless, our dreams allow us to express what or how we really think or feel about things.

Dreams can be a way of facing your fears head-on and dealing with uncomfortable situations that occur in your everyday life. For instance, if you face your fear in a battle in your dream-life, you are more likely to feel prepared to overcome an obstacle or fear in the real world. In a way, your dream-life is where you put the 'practice' in and mentally assure yourself that you can do it. Of course, imagination plays a big role in this. For example, you may assume that a person is upset with you for one reason or another. And upon awakening, after having dreamt about them, you may react to them in a certain way that you wouldn't consciously do in real life. Thus, in this case, your dreams can act like a stage or playground where it is a 'safe' place to explore and express our feelings. The reality may actually be completely different, and perhaps the person in question doesn't have any disagreements with you whatsoever.

Although, at times, particularly if you are intuitive, it is possible that you may have picked up on something or vibe from the other person, and therefore, in this case, your dream can appear like a warning.

Warnings or premonitions can also come through dreams. You may have even experienced this for yourself. An example of this is when one person in a romantic relationship mistrusts a partner for one reason or another but can't quite put a finger on why. Sometimes, ideas can surface in a dream, and if it feels real enough, the dreamer automatically begins to look for real-life evidence as a way to justify the behaviour or dream. In most cases, it could indeed be simply a dream, but now and again, there may be an element of truth to it. Unfortunately, a person may discover that a partner is cheating after having dreamt about it. Of course, the opposite may also be true: the dreamer is the person who is committing the infidelity and is portraying the innocent party as the person behind the deceit. In other words, deflecting the blame onto the other.

There is also another kind of dream that seems more real. Vivid dreams can seem as though they are really happening, particularly if they are sad dreams like dreams of someone close to you dying. Sometimes it can be a relief to awake from your dream because you know that it was just a dream and have nothing to worry about. Many scientists put this down to physical reasons, such as the foods you eat just before you go to bed like cheese or chocolate. Alcohol can also affect this and so can illness and any other prescribed medication you may have taken. Watching dramatic programmes before you fall asleep won't help either because some can be very disturbing and promote fear during the night. While all these are factors to take into account, sometimes there may be a genuine underlying message behind the dream.

Let dreams help you in your life. Your dreams can be a magical

89

place where you really believe
that positive things can happen.
They are a place where you can be
your own hero or heroine; where
life is just how you want it and
you are successful. Your mind is a
remarkable gift, which can act as
a resource and be trained to
create true wonders. In fact, your
mind could be thought of as the
eighth wonder of the world
because its gifts are unlimited.

Allow yourself to dream
without limits, and do not worry
about how you should think or
feel while you are dreaming.
Dreams are a beautiful outlet, so
you do not have to store
everything up in your head and
constantly be thinking about a
problem. In a way, it is a great
stress-reliever as it releases
unnecessary pressure from your
mind.

Then there are the inspirational dreams; these are my favourite type of dreams. Many artists receive inspiration from their dreams. They may have a dream that drives them to take action when they awake. Writers, including myself, also become inspired while they sleep and even awake during the night to write ideas down in case they forget them in the morning. This is popular among musicians and many creative people. Sometimes you can hear words or receive most of your ideas in the still of the night. It is when you allow those ideas to surface that the magic happens.

You may also discover a lot about yourself when you dream. You realise how you see yourself. Do you see yourself as someone strong or someone who fades into the background? Your mind may even prompt some questions to help identify more of your thoughts and feelings about this. For instance, do you wish you were braver? Slimmer? Healthier?

Once you get a clear understanding of how you feel about these thoughts, this will inevitably instigate you to do something about them. So, start by taking the first steps to become more like the person you want to be. This could mean becoming a healthier, stronger, or a more confident version of yourself.

Dreams have a way of teaching us what we do or don't want out of life. This applies to good dreams or nightmares. We all have different wants and needs; what may seem like a nightmare to you, may be paradise to someone else.

There are of course dreams that are purely there for

entertainment. Have fun with these and enjoy them. It is always good to keep a sense of humour about life. I often awake from a dream giggling.

Dreams are very telling and can speak volumes. Take the time to listen to them. What messages are your dreams trying to tell you?

Chapter 10

YOUR REALITY

Reality is an extraordinary concept. What appears as one person's reality may be completely different from another's. This is because we each perceive things in a different way.

Take two witnesses in an investigation. How one person explains an event can be reported differently from how the other person remembers it. Each may observe different details or events. For instance, if you see a young guy wearing a hoodie running and an old lady with a bag in front of him, you may quickly assume that the guy is

going to try and steal from her
while another person could think
he is running to catch a bus,
which has just pulled up. It all
depends on how we interpret a
situation.

You may be familiar with the
scenario of a glass filled halfway
with water. While one person may
see the glass as half-full, another
may see it as half-empty. This
also occurs in everyday
situations. For instance, if there is
a train delay, one person might
sit and complain about it, while
another might use it as an
opportunity to make a phone call
or catch-up on some reading.
Granted, there may be other
factors involved, such as a
person's mood on a particular
day, but, regardless of the outside
factors, we are all different. This
means we each think differently,

so is it any wonder that we see things differently?

Some may be accused of 'living in a bubble'. This is usually implied as a negative comment from people who view themselves as 'realists' and others as dreamers. But in reality, it is only their personal opinion. While it is great to keep informed of everyday current affairs and what's going on around you, it can also be quite destructive to constantly focus your attention on all the negative influences around you.

As with most things in life, balance is the key. Stay informed but learn to switch yourself off from it too. Otherwise, you will find yourself unnecessarily drained from all the things going on around you. Drama can be like a merry-go-round that continues to spin. If you are not careful, you'll get caught up in it and lose sight of yourself and what you truly desire.

There are many people who are only too quick to judge others. They stand on the side-lines and criticise and condemn other people's behaviour because they do not have the courage to do things themselves. Instead, they prefer to gossip and put others down. I bet these people are not the happiest people inside. If they were, they wouldn't feel the need to judge others by their own standards.

Unfortunately, it is virtually impossible to avoid people of this mindset, so instead, try to keep the peace and learn to live with them. The good thing is that if you aim to feel good about yourself the majority of the time and maintain a positive attitude, you will quickly discover who these people are and equip yourself with the knowledge that they are only really making themselves miserable. Don't entertain their opinions or negative thoughts for too long, and don't let them bring you down. If you can, keep the conversation short and sweet and move on or spend as little time as possible with them.

Many people have dreams that just stay dreams. This could be because they doubt that they can become part of their reality or believe that they happen to others and not to them. We tend to get what we believe in. If you think this way, you have a choice: You can either continue to be this way or you can start to change your thought pattern by thinking and looking at things differently. To help you begin the transformation of turning your dreams into reality, try the visualisation exercise in Chapter 4. Then proceed to the next step which involves getting practical. This could be doing some research, working out your finances, or writing a step-by-step process of how you will achieve it. Including a time frame can also help because this will drive you to take action by a certain time.

Throughout the process, you need to stay positive and remain as focused as possible. In other words, you need to keep a strong mind, and this takes practice and consistency. Do things that work for you, whether that is prayer, meditation, visualising, or simply daydreaming about what you'd like to achieve.

Patience and persistence are required with all of this. Contrary to popular belief, very few things happen overnight, despite appearing as if they do. Keep following your heart and your passion, and above all, believe in your dreams and yourself.

This is your reality, and it is up to you to make the effort and put the work in. This may involve more than just physical work; it could include mental work too. For instance, being a positive person in a room full of negative people can be challenging, especially when it can take all your energy and focus to stand firm in your beliefs and positive thoughts.

The good thing is that when you usually start taking the steps towards turning your dreams into reality, you usually receive a helping hand. God and the laws of attraction have a way of moving things along a bit (i.e. things start falling into place), and you may meet the

connections you need to propel
your dream forward in a way you
never expected.

Make your reality positive,
supportive, uplifting, and full of
love. A place where your dreams
really can come true.

Chapter 11

MANIFESTING

Attracting what you want in life usually begins with an intention or a declaration that you want something to happen. This could be a change in your lifestyle, a house, a car, a partner in life, a business you'd love, a place you would like to visit, and many other desires. Since it is your vision and your life, there aren't any limits unless you place them there yourself.

Setting an intention is the first step towards manifesting or making your desired vision become reality. For once you set your intention, you can move forward with it. It is not unusual to start finding synchronicities. For instance, you may meet someone who can be instrumental in connecting you with a person who can help make things happen. Or a house you have had your heart set on to buy suddenly becomes available to purchase.

You may also find that you mysteriously receive the exact amount of money you require to get your business venture off the ground or you may discover that your dream house is affordable after all. Things have a way of coming together.

A good way of attracting things to you is to act as if you already have your desired outcome. Step into the feeling of it and notice every single detail (i.e. the scent, taste, touch, and people around you). What can you see? Become part of it as though you have it right now.

Or if you don't have it now, prepare and plan for it. If you want to move to a lovely house, start buying little things for it and design how your room will be in detail. Consider the colours, fabrics, and textures. Plan the layout of the room. Imagine having people there at a party or gathering.

When you can tap into the details of it all, it makes it all the more real. You may even begin to feel the urge to speed things up. This is what is often referred to as the high-vibration frequency inside you. This builds up the momentum and encourages you to move forward with plans in a big way. The more this happens, the faster things start happening, which makes it all the more exciting. Excitement is infectious, and once you start embracing this, you will not only feel differently, but your enthusiasm will shine through you. Others around you will start to see your eyes sparkle with joy, and they will probably want in on it. It is almost like a best-kept secret that only few experience but many yearn for.

This brings on a snowball effect, as when you manifest one thing, it attracts something else and so forth. Just like everything, it may take practise and perseverance, and you may not receive everything straightaway. There will be times when you will need to trust in the higher wisdom and greater good because we don't always know what is best for us. We may think we do, but sometimes things happen for a reason, and if you don't receive exactly what you want, you may receive something better in the long run. For instance, you could suddenly be made redundant due to unforeseen circumstances. This may come as a shock to you at first but could be the perfect opportunity to do something you have always wanted to do, such as travel around the world or start a business. Although you may not completely understand why, this will become apparent in the future, so take heart and be full of courage.

Putting your trust in something unseen isn't always easy, and it will take patience and understanding. Sometimes you may simply have an inner-knowing that all is well and the right thing will happen at the right time. Have faith and move on with certainty and hope.

Having some hope in the future is better than having no hope at all.

Believe in possibilities. There are too many people walking around with unfulfilled dreams and possibly even resentment. This is probably due to them listening to doubts along the way. Why is it that the majority of people tend to believe the doubts more than in themselves? Negative talk can be to blame. This happens all too often. Instead, we should be giving life and ourselves a chance to make our dreams come true. If we do not try, how will we ever know?

When you do manifest something in your reality, have gratitude in your heart and use it as an example for others if you feel inclined. It is so important to celebrate all that you have accomplished. In sharing your happy moments, you are indirectly helping others feel happier about themselves too because you are opening their minds, eyes, and even their hearts to possibilities that they would otherwise have not known if it were not for you. Tell the world what has been accomplished or at least your small portion of the world. In doing so, you will uplift others.

You can have that dream lifestyle, build a beautiful business, move into your dream house, and drive that gorgeous sports car if you want to. Just believe you can, feel you can, and act as if you already have it, and you will soon start sending out those positive vibes, which will start attracting these or similar things to you. As long as everything is done out of love and with good intentions, then

there is no reason why you cannot
manifest with ease.

Chapter 12

YOUR BELIEFS

As I have mentioned before, what you believe about yourself affects every part of you: how you think about yourself, how you carry yourself, and how you are perceived by others.

You may not realise the great impact it has at first. It is often easier to observe others than ourselves. For instance, you may notice how people walk into a room, whether they stand tall and walk with confidence or if they immediately look down, enter a room with slouched shoulders, and do not want anybody to notice them. Ironically, in a room full of boldness, the not-so-bold stand out even more. What you notice about people speaks volumes. For instance, it is obvious that they don't think highly of themselves and they may not think what they have to say is important and would rather agree with others rather than state their own opinions. It may have also become a habit for them to fade into the background, and they may feel more comfortable that way. Perhaps you can relate to this.

The good news is that it's not too late for you to do something about this. It all starts with what you think about yourself and how that makes you feel.

Earlier I talked about the effect your thoughts have on your words and your actions. Well, your beliefs are very close to your thoughts. In a way, they are the practical element of your thoughts; they are what provoke passion in you to move forward because your beliefs are what you feel is true about yourself, others, and the things around you. Beliefs are also strong feelings that you have in regards to your faith, political choices, environmental choices, etc. They can affect decisions you make in everyday life, such as whether you become a vegetarian, decide not to wear fur, or avoid certain situations. They are usually what you feel passionate about and have strong feelings for. In summary, your beliefs say a lot about you as an individual or as part of a community.

You may not even be aware of what your beliefs are. You may think that you are quite laid-back, and then all of a sudden, something may occur that triggers you, and you can't understand why.

For instance, if you have a partner and an attractive person walks into a room who starts chatting to your significant other, you may immediately feel annoyed and perhaps a little jealous. This could trigger a memory, such as one where a sibling or someone in your class at school got more attention than you did or took something from you. You may find yourself making an uncharacteristically nasty comment; this is your way of retaliating. It is surprising what you can discover when you find your buttons have been pushed. You tend to find out what really makes you tick because what triggers emotions also enables you to find out what you feel strongly about. It's amazing what you can learn about yourself when the heat is on. You are fascinating and have hidden depths. Not everyone knows themselves completely inside and out. Something you had no idea you felt so passionate about may be exposed when you least expect it. Be prepared for the truth to unfold.

Take the time to get to know yourself. Pick up a journal or notebook and gently notice your thoughts, opinions, and reactions over a week, no matter how small. It could be an opinion about a television programme or an article you read in a newspaper. Make a note of how you feel towards the topics and the type of decisions you make. You may be pleasantly surprised and even discover things you never realised you thought so strongly about.

115

After you have done this exercise, casually read through it. Try to remain as neutral as possible and ask yourself: 'If I were reading about someone who had these thoughts for the first time, how would I describe the person? Would it be opinionated, easy-going, fussy, critical, confident, or naïve?'

This may start to paint a picture of how you appear, first to yourself and then to others. Are you surprised by your responses? Write down your thoughts about your responses and how they make you feel. How do you feel about yourself now?

Your results may even shock you. Don't worry about this; it is perfectly natural to be surprised at what you find. On the other hand, you may find you are not surprised at all. There are no right or wrong answers. There are only your answers.

Once you have made this discovery, you can start going through each response and ask yourself why you think this way or have this opinion. Is it because you have adopted or learnt this opinion from your parents or caregivers or have you always thought this way? This is a good exercise to find out more about yourself and how your original beliefs have come about. For instance, have you been taught that having one opinion is right and another is wrong or have you come to this conclusion yourself? You may be surprised to learn how many ideas you have adopted from others and how many are actually your own.

If you find that the majority of your beliefs are what you have adopted from others, it may be a good idea to go through whether you still personally believe them to be true now or if you have changed your mind. There is nothing wrong with changing your opinion and beliefs about things. We are always developing and growing; what you once believed to be true as a child may no longer serve you as an adult.

The main thing is to know what you truly believe in. This is a basis of your strength of character. You will indeed now know who you really are and what you truly believe. This will have an impact on your whole being; it will show through in your words, your manner, how you hold yourself, your posture, and how you walk into a room. In effect, your beliefs will shine through and shape your actions and how others perceive you. It will bring about an air of certainty and confidence as you remain true to yourself and your beliefs.

Chapter 13

EXPECTATIONS

What you expect to happen often has a way of becoming true. Remember how the glass is either half-empty or half-full? This relates to mindset and our perception of ourselves and those around us. There is also the idea that if you don't expect too much, then you won't be disappointed. This thought is usually linked with the need to protect oneself and often used as a defence mechanism.

Some people may even feel guilty about expecting great outcomes. This could be due to the ideas they have learnt or adopted while growing up. It's amazing just how many of your parents' opinions and values get passed onto you without you even realising it.

For instance, as a teenager, you may disagree wholeheartedly with your parent over a topic, such as a particular diet you want to follow, and then, later in life when you yourself are a parent, you completely understand where your parents were coming from, and you may even find yourself repeating the phrases they used to say. In a way, 'the penny has dropped', and all has become clear to you. When I was a teenager, I thought I knew it all and that my parents didn't know what they were talking about because they were of a different age group. Now that I have reached a similar age group as my parents were, I realise that experience counts for a lot and perhaps I should have paid a little more attention.

I remember I used to stick up for my favourite pop group on the TV when my parents used to say that they were on drugs. I recall really getting annoyed and arguing with them. However, later on in life, after watching a replay of their older performances, I could see how they were indeed so obviously on drugs, and it had even been reported in the newspapers about their drug addictions and how one of the members almost died due to his drug habits.

This was a complete revelation to me as I used to believe everything I read about them, which positioned them in a good light to gain better publicity.

We can also pick up both high and low expectations from our parents. For instance, if you are often pessimistic, it is likely that you picked this up from a parent and may have been inclined to agree with them. An example of this is if one of your parents often blamed others for his or her circumstances, you may feel inclined to steer towards this idea, particularly if you go for a job interview and it wasn't successful.

On the other hand, if your parents are go-getters and have a positive and can-do attitude, you are more likely to feel that you can accomplish anything in life and look for opportunities wherever you go instead of excuses. For example, if you didn't make the sports team one year, you may decide to practise more often and improve your technique so you can try again the following year and get into the team.

There is of course the option that your parents were a mixture of the two. Perhaps one was more positive while the other looked out for the pitfalls and steered towards playing it safe and settled for what is. This is good to know because then you get a glimpse of both worlds and can make an informed choice by looking at both sides. For instance, if one side of your family always has plenty of money and thrives while the other side seems to be always waiting for their next payday, this can teach you the importance of budgeting, so that you always have a steady flow of income.

When you expect a negative outcome, you are preparing for failure mentally and physically. If you think about this strongly, it will inevitably affect the actions you take, and the outcome is more likely to be negative. This could be because internally you are trying to justify your belief or expectations so you can say to yourself or those around you: 'See? I told you so.' For instance, if you expect to forget your lines at a school play, then it actually happens.

On the other hand, if you expect an optimistic outcome, you are more likely to give yourself an internal 'pep talk', which will influence your thoughts in an encouraging way and have a positive effect on your actions. Others may also notice that you are more determined or simply want something more. These factors are more likely to lead to success.

Expecting the best and feeling positive usually has an expansive feel about it. In other words, it gives you space to grow and come up with options and exciting ideas that often lead to opportunities. This can be displayed in your posture; for instance, you may tend to look straight ahead with your shoulders back and appear confident, whereas being negative has a limiting feeling and energy behind it. This is why people who feel negative are inclined to withdraw more, and this is usually displayed by looking down as if in defeat.

You may have noticed this in others. For instance, some people make excuses for why they can't do something, whether it's because they require more money or more time. They may even blame someone else.

Look for examples of positive behaviour in others. For example, sports champions expect to win and base their whole training, fitness routine, diet, and thought patterns towards expecting to win. Failure doesn't enter their minds at all. They not only train physically but mentally. Sometimes mentality can be the hardest hurdle to overcome because they are familiar with the physical activity, but mental training on the other hand is a whole different ball game.

For instance, imagine getting up to train outside at five a.m. in the morning if it is pouring with rain and freezing cold. Most people would turn over and go back to sleep or make a ton of excuses for not going outside. But, an athlete has to put mind over matter and literally 'psyche' up to do it. It takes determination and discipline to stick to a tight schedule, and nine times out of ten, the athlete is happy to endure the task. Perhaps not always during the process, but most certainly after achieving a successful result. It's as though a personal test and an obstacle has been overcome. The feeling of accomplishment is great. It also affects others who see this, as they probably wonder how it was done and wish they could do it too. It has a positive impact by showing others that everyone can achieve what they set out to, which is a fantastic example to set, particularly for younger people.

While the majority of people make excuses, champions make a difference.

A champion can come in all different forms. It could be a mother picking up and praising a child on his or her way home from school, a lollipop man or lady helping people across the road, a young person going for their first job, someone starting a business, or a neighbour helping their neighbour out. You can find champions everywhere if you look for them. Observe people in your everyday world and see for yourself.

When you set an intention of something you want, expect to receive it. Go even further than that: Believe you have received it and imagine how it makes you feel and the impact you can bring to others around you by feeling this way.

Fill your heart and mind with positive expectations, thoughts and prepare for success. When you expect miracles and success, you are more likely to receive them.

Chapter 14

MAGNET OF LOVE

We each have a presence, whether we realise it or not. There are days when we don't feel up to much and prefer to keep a low profile, and there are days when we want to shout out from the rooftops and tell the world how wonderful we are feeling.

One way of discovering the effect you have on those around you is to notice your energy regardless of how you are feeling. Write down your observations over a week and then look back on them. You may find that a pattern emerges or that there are certain times of the day when you feel better than others. Of course, there are other factors to take into account. For instance, the weather, the season, the people you are with, and the location you are in can have an impact. However, all of these factors have a common denominator: You.

Have you ever realised or felt your inner presence? Or have you ever felt your inner power? We all have an inner strength; sometimes we may not even realise it until there is no alternative but to tap into it. This could be due to an unfortunate circumstance or life event, but it doesn't have to be.

Sometimes it is easier to see someone else's strength as opposed to your own. For instance, you walk into a room and see a person standing up on stage, and it appears that the audience is in the palm of his or her hand and hanging on their every word. Yes, it could be due to charisma and experience, but it may also be due to the skill and ability acquired by learning to tap into inner strength and radiate an inner presence. What we don't often realise is that many things can be learnt, including speaking to a crowd.

You may have read that everything has energy, whether it's in a physical or mental form. Even a thought process is made up of energy, which is transformed into vibrations, and helps to bring things into action. This has been experienced by many people a number of times, hence the school of thought behind the law of attraction and metaphysics. The mind has significant influence over the body, which has been proven when people who have been ill for a very long time suddenly recover when they put their minds to it. Even patients who have been in a coma for months can suddenly awaken. Our minds are more powerful than we realise.

We have energy around us all the time, and we also emit energy from us. Try it for yourself and see: Rub your hands together for a short time, and then place them at an equal distance apart. Notice the feeling you get when your palms face each other. Start off with your palms facing each other and then slowly bring them apart a little. Or rub the palms of your hands together, touch a fully-blown balloon, and feel the energy between your palm and the balloon. Yes, it's a form of static, and it is also a form of energy.

The more aware you become of yourself, the more you realise

the strength you have inside of you, which can affect others around you. Like most things, this has to be practised on a regular basis. Although, just being aware of it can have a tremendous effect.

Here is an exercise to help you become more self-aware:

Shut down all distractions, turn off your phone, close the door, and make sure you can't be disturbed. Close your eyes, and visualise a warm, soft golden light grow larger in the inside of your heart. Envision it slowly expanding until it covers your torso and then slowly covering your entire body. Think of it like a large circle outside your body.

Now, see yourself in your mind's eye inside the circle with your arm outstretched. Feel this warm, loving energy becoming larger until it covers the area you live in, the continent you are in, and then the entire planet. Feel all the positive energy and love.

Then slowly begin to draw it in with the circle becoming smaller and smaller until you have it right back in your heart. Imagine it becoming smaller again until the next time you need to draw upon it. Say a prayer and thank God for the power of love.

When you feel this golden light and fill your heart with love, you will naturally become a magnet of love and of light. You will be naturally drawn to all the beauty in the world, and others will enjoy being in your presence. You will feel calm and happy and have a sense of peace wherever you are. It's almost like bringing calm to a troubled soul. It's like finding yourself in 'soft' times rather than feeling the harshness of 'hard' times. You can tell you are in 'hard' time when nothing seems to be going right and you feel like you are having a bad day. For instance, you may drop some eggs or miss your bus to work.

However, when you are in a 'soft' time, everything seems to fall into place and flows beautifully. You don't need to hustle or try too hard. You can simply just enjoy being in a state of grace and tranquillity. You have a sense of self-assuredness about you that others find refreshing and wish they could have it. Life is quite simply a joy.

When you are in this moment of bliss, you never want it to end. But, of course, you need to draw your energy and ground yourself too so that you are able to go on and have the energy to continue the work you need to do in life. If you keep giving out your energy, you may feel depleted and not feel your usual self, which is why it is important to pay attention to when you need to withdraw and rest, so you can expand when you need it most. It's a little like how the waves of the ocean appear from a bird's eye view: The waves go out and seem to expand, and then they go in and appear to gain strength and motion.

As they say, what you give out, you will get back, just like the ebb and flow of the ocean. Be a magnet of all things good, such as love, kindness, peace, and prosperity. Above all, be a magnet of love.

Chapter 15

LUCK AND OPPORTUNITY

Do you believe in luck? Being lucky can mean different things to different people. For some, it could mean being at the right place at the right time. To others, it is when things occur that they never thought would ever happen, like winning the lottery or a competition. Then there is the other philosophy of believing that you make your own luck or the harder you work, the luckier you get.

For me, I think luck is a feeling you get. It's almost like

you know something good is about to happen. It can bring a smile to your face, and it is almost like an 'inner knowing'. It is something that you know and no one else does. Luck in itself is a belief. If you believe in having good luck, it is more likely to happen. Like most beliefs, this can be learnt from your parents or from the people you grew up with. If one of your parents believed that he or she is lucky, it is more likely that you will adopt this thought pattern. The opposite is also true. If a parent strongly disagrees with luck and that you have to work hard for everything in life, then the child is most likely to take on these beliefs.

However, this doesn't always have to be the case. You can decide to feel lucky. It may sound simple, and it is. You can choose what to believe in. You may have noticed that the people who seem lucky usually believe that they are. You accomplish what you believe in. That's why successful people believe in what they achieve. They may not succeed every single time, but when they don't, they learn from it and try a different strategy and explore what went wrong to minimise the risk of it happening again. The same is true of people who do not accomplish what they set out to. They may blame it on having bad luck or focus on the odds that were against them. You may have heard the saying 'you get what you focus on'. Well, this goes for you believing in luck as well.

Luck could also be considered as something you develop like a skill. For instance, the more times you do a task, the more likely you are to improve at it. Practise makes it better and instils more confidence in you. The more confident you feel often goes hand in hand with how lucky you feel. To feel 'lucky' requires an element of trust in your own ability. This can also transfer to the 'vibes' you send out to those around you. A 'vibe' is a feeling or atmosphere that is created. Ever had a feeling about someone after he or she had just walked into a room? This could be due to the 'vibes' the person was giving out and that you picked up. The more positive vibes you send out, the more you attract good energy into your life. These can materialise into positive thoughts and successful outcomes.

Have you ever woken up first thing in the morning with a feeling that something wonderful is on the horizon? You can feel it in the air that it will be a good day and everything is going to go your way. Well, I bet you feel lucky on days like this. Not only do you feel lucky, you attract positive energy and things to you. You may get that parking space easily, get a discount on your shopping, or receive money you were not expecting. Days like these are a godsend. When you get these days, hold on to this feeling as long as you can. This increases the chances of feeling like this more often. It is a little like tapping into a secret resource or finding a hidden treasure. Once you get it, you want more of the same because it feels so good.

This hidden reserve of portable, golden energy can also rub off on those around you. They see the effect it has on you and want some for themselves. I recall this after winning a holiday to Greece. I told my manager at the time, and he couldn't believe it.

He immediately touched my arm and told the other staff to touch my arm for good luck. They all wanted the good luck to rub off onto them. It was quite a funny scene.

Opportunity is often linked to luck. The more open you are to receiving opportunities, the more you will attract them, and the more opportunities you take, the luckier you will appear. Look out for opportunities wherever you are because they could happen in the least expected places.

You do need to have the right frame of mind in the first place to identify them as opportunities instead of challenges. Sometimes if you see them as work or a challenge, it may have a negative effect and won't feel so good, whereas if you see it as an opportunity, the feeling is much lighter and far more positive and has an air of success about it. For instance, a client contacts you and needs something done urgently, and you are very busy because you are preparing to go away. Instead of seeing it as an upheaval, try seeing it as an opportunity to help someone out. This will shift your whole perception of it and enable you to feel good about being able to help him or her.

Aim to feel positive as often as possible. This means believing in yourself and having confidence and trusting in your own abilities. You have got to believe in yourself wholeheartedly in order to feel the positive energy inside before it can overflow and have a positive influence on those around you.

Of course, you can make more opportunities for yourself just by showing up in more places where opportunities can present themselves. Perhaps you can go to events, parties, and social situations where you are more likely to meet people who can offer these opportunities. Paying attention and listening to others can also help as you never know what knowledge may come in handy. You can help others in the process if you are more willing to share your expertise.

When these opportunities arise, remember that first impressions are important; it usually takes a matter of seconds to make a first impression. So how people perceive you can go a long way towards opening doors for you, which are basically opportunities you haven't explored yet.

There are opportunities all around us if we look for them. Instead of walking around and only seeing what is close at hand, we could open our hearts and look for the beauty around us.

This includes the beauty in others too. You may glance at something once, but if you take a look for a moment longer, you may see things differently.

Opportunities can arise when you least expect them. It could be when you are walking down the road, popping into a coffee shop, or during a conversation with a stranger on the phone. Keep a look out for them and make the most of them when they do come. Opportunities are like gifts; they can come in all different forms. Just because they don't arrive wrapped in beautiful paper with a satin ribbon, doesn't mean that they aren't gifts.

In a nutshell, the two go hand in hand: when you increase your opportunities, you increase your luck.

Chapter 16

SURRENDER

In these modern times, it is natural for us to want to control everything. We control what we eat, drink, where we go, and the clothes we wear. Many of us feel that if we don't have control over a situation or outcome, it is the end of the world. You may know or even be someone who likes to do the same when you are on holiday. You choose the exact destination, precise flight times, location of flight seats, and hotel rooms. I have to admit, I often do this.

But what would happen if you just went with 'the flow' for a change? You may think it would be a disaster and everything would fall apart, but the reality may be somewhat different if you let it.

Have you ever had one of those days where you just 'be' and see what happens along the way? A day where you don't make any plans and just simply 'go with the flow'? I bet you have. Although those days may be few and far between, they can make all the difference.

Sometimes surrendering to 'what is' can feel like a breath of fresh air; it is almost like a holiday. The hardest part is allowing ourselves to be that way and just let go.

The truth of it is that we cannot control everyone, everything, and every situation or outcome, no matter how hard we try. It would be better for us in the long run, and especially beneficial to our health and minds, if we stopped trying to. It doesn't matter how much we try to convince ourselves otherwise; sometimes things can seem so frustrating and the more we try and control something, the harder it is. Sound familiar?

There may be times when the more you try to get things to go your way, the more they resist and will not budge. A solution to this is to not try so hard.

Try to relax and accept things as they are once in a while. You will discover a lighter energy around you and may even start to enjoy this feeling. You see, life doesn't have to be a struggle and a challenge all the time—unless you make it that way. As with most things, this could simply be changing a habit that you have had for many years. You may have inherited the feeling of the need to control everything or you may have learnt this behaviour from another adult when you were a child; it makes no difference how you learnt it. All you need to do is to replace it with a new habit: the habit of surrender.

Surrendering doesn't have to feel like you're giving up. In fact, it could mean that you are doing the opposite. Just because you try something new doesn't mean you are a victim and that you are admitting defeat in some way. By changing your perspective and way of doing things, you may even find you are bringing more happiness to a situation.

For example, it is common knowledge that couples have more arguments during the holiday season than any other season. More often than not, arguments arise when one person demands control over another, and the other person becomes defensive. I wonder how many of these arguments could have been resolved or even avoided if the people involved decided to relax and go with the flow a little or, as a last resort, at least agreed to disagree.

Relationships don't have to be a battleground, particularly on holiday when you could be spending quality time with each other instead of being at loggerheads with one another. For instance, if one person wanted to go shopping and another prefers to visit a museum, perhaps you could both compromise, and each go on a separate excursion and meet up afterwards. That way, you both will have something interesting to tell each other when you next see each other, and this also avoids any resentment towards one another.

A life event can also be a stressful time, especially as humans don't necessarily like change, despite what others say. Most people prefer things to stay the same, but life isn't like that. What if we didn't choose to worry about things so much? Better still, what if we chose to surrender to what life has in store for us instead?

Regardless of your beliefs, life is meant to be full of joy, happiness, and love, if we allow it. Most of the time, it is us who stand in our own way. God wants us to experience all the good things in life. Some of these may be missed if we insist on controlling everything. We need to accept that there may be times in our lives when we don't always know what is best for us. We may fool ourselves into thinking we do but think of how many times you have made a bad decision at some point in your life. You are only human; it's okay to make mistakes, and it is also okay to have fun and be adventurous once in a while.

The world is full of possibilities, and instead of spending your time looking at every detail and looking for faults, let's enjoy the time we have and dare to live in the moment now and again. It would make a pleasant change. Who knows? You may even surprise yourself.

Make a new start and have a fresh outlook. Stop looking down and searching for faults when you walk down the road and try looking upwards and see all the good life has to offer instead. You could listen to the birds singing, feel the warmth on your skin from a summer breeze, or watch the shops bustle with activity (this is a good sign of how the economy is thriving around you). You may even inspire others around you and build an atmosphere of positive encouragement and optimism. Having a good atmosphere will make the world a better place and more fun to be in.

So, surrender to what if and accept what is because you never know what surprises are awaiting you.

Chapter 17

LISTEN TO YOUR HEART

When you do things out of love and with an open heart, which means being accepting of others and all the good things around you, you are likely to accomplish more. You will feel happier and have a much more positive feeling and approach to what you are doing. There will be a lighter feeling about you, which is encouraging, and you will also find that you are enjoying the process. It could even be fun.

Try and pay attention to what your heart is telling you. As I mentioned previously in Chapter

7, take the time to become quiet and listen. I mean really listen. You know when you are on the right path because things will just 'feel' right, and everything just seems to fall into place without tremendous amounts of effort.

You may meet the right acquaintance who can help you connect with someone, stumble upon an idea or plan that can be easily put into action, or you may find the right tool or software you can use to help you complete a task. Everything will just flow.

The opposite can be said if you are heading down the wrong path. It can feel very frustrating when nothing seems to be going right, no matter what you do. You may feel as though someone has let you down or find something too difficult to resolve. Nothing makes sense, and what 'should' work in theory doesn't seem to work in practice. It is easy to beat yourself up over it and think of yourself as a failure, but before you step into victim-mode, stop!

Take some time out to do something completely different: go for a walk, read a magazine, meet with a friend, or watch a film. Do something you enjoy. A lot of times, when we step away from a situation, it helps us to reconnect with ourselves and our heart. We are allowing ourselves to feel the love we deserve by being true to ourselves and doing things just because they make us feel good. This switches the 'feel good' receptors in our minds, which invites more of the same feelings to us. And when we feel this good, we attract good things to us in every way. We become more relaxed and, therefore, less defensive. We don't try so hard, and things naturally fall into place. Things start getting good again because we have reminded ourselves of what is truly important. This isn't always easy at first because we have to learn to let go and let them be. But the more times we do this, the more it makes sense because we feel better about things. So, if you ever feel stuck and think that things are not going the way you hoped, take some time out before you step back into the situation; it can have an amazing impact.

Everyone likes to feel loved and appreciated, but we need to feel this way about ourselves first before we start looking to others for support. When you get to know yourself and really listen to how your heart is feeling about things, it can make all the difference in the world. Start from within and take a moment to listen and take in what you hear before putting it out into the world. Your inner guidance, as described in Chapter 7, is a combination of your heart, mind, and soul. Trust what you hear and how you feel instead of always looking to others for support. First, start supporting yourself by looking within and rediscover what you already have. You may be surprised to find that you already have more to offer than you ever thought possible.

When you speak or write from the heart, others can tell. For instance, when someone gives a speech, it is easy to tell the difference between reading and speaking from a script, in comparison to truly believing in what is being said and meaning every word. There is feeling behind it and you can hear the passion in the voice and see it in

161

the eyes. His or her body language will also resonate with the message. People will be drawn to this and feel connected in some way. Speak out of love and from the heart. Hearts connect to hearts.

Your heart will never lie to you. Your mind may play tricks, you can pretend things are alright when they are not; and even logic can be manipulated at times, so you hear what you want to hear. For example, in an unhappy romantic relationship, you could try to see things differently or even think differently, but these practices can often be short-lived. There is no mistaking, your true feelings always have a way of revealing themselves, and no matter how hard you try to hide them they have a habit of coming out in one way or another. This may be when you least expect.

For instance, you may suddenly fly into a rage over your spouse throwing an item of clothing on the floor after you have told them a number of times to put clothes in either the laundry basket or hang it up and not disrespect you after all the effort you put into keeping a nice, tidy home.

To save yourself a lot of time, pain, and heartache, trust what you feel and communicate them when necessary. Allow yourself to check-in and be in tune with how you are truly feeling. There is no point in kidding yourself and thinking things are okay when they are far from it. It is just yourself you are fooling. If you stay true to yourself and your feelings, you will have far more love, joy, and success, and in turn, you will be in a position to bring more love, warmth, and happiness to others around you because what you are offering will come from a good place. It will come from your heart, and that is worth more than most material things.

You deserve all these beautiful things, and the sooner you start listening to your heart, the sooner you will experience all the goodness life has to offer you. What is your heart telling you?

Chapter 18

PREPARE

Preparation goes hand in hand with acting as if something wonderful is about to happen. Rather than just mentally preparing for something great to enter your life, try to also make physical preparations. This way you are sending out positive vibes out to the world that you are ready for this in your life and you are making space for it.

For instance, if you want a new wardrobe full of beautiful clothes, begin by decluttering your existing wardrobe. Go through it meticulously, and hold each item of clothing up to you, or try it on if you prefer. Look at yourself with the item in front of the mirror and ask yourself if you truly feel amazing in it. Does it make you feel happy? If it doesn't, then throw it out or donate it to charity so it can bring happiness to someone else. You'll be surprised at how much lighter you feel afterwards. This is making space for clothes that will bring you joy and help you feel good about yourself. Don't worry about how you are going to get these new pieces, just enjoy this new, refreshing feeling.

If you would like to entertain more friends at home, then clear your environment of anything that feels dated or worse for wear and look for pieces of home furnishings or décor that are more welcoming and up-to-date. Perhaps purchase a new dinner set with the number of plates representing the number of people you would love to have over. Clear some clutter and make space so that your home is ready to receive your guests.

I recall before purchasing our first house how I just casually glanced at the newspaper and started feeling drawn to a particular road full of delightful houses. I remember thinking at the time how wonderful it would be to live there. I even imagined walking home from work down the same road. Not long after, we checked our finances and found that it would be possible to buy a home. We had a viewing at a different house and as if by chance, it got cancelled and the estate agent said she had another property that had just come up not far from where we were. We visited the place and discovered it was on the same road where I first looked in the newspaper. When we arrived, we both immediately fell in love with the place. It even had my taste in décor and the exact wallpaper I had chosen for it! It was readymade for us. We made an offer a little lower than the asking price, and to our delight, it was accepted. I worked it out later and discovered that it was exactly six months after I first saw it in the newspaper. The timing couldn't have been better for us.

This technique can be applied to any goal or dream you'd like to accomplish. When you prepare, go through it in the smallest detail; for instance, if you would love a new home, imagine the furniture you would like, the colour of walls, and how you like your furniture set out. Then write it down. The more details you have the better; because this allows excitement to build, which in turn triggers your mind to believe and expect it, and therefore making it more likely to happen. Don't worry about how or when. God has a way of taking care of that side of things.

You may also find that you start feeling excited about it and that it actually feels real. That's because your mind doesn't know the difference; it doesn't distinguish make-believe from reality. Your imagination has already begun creating this event, so it is inevitable that it is going to happen. When you get to this stage, it is imperative that you do not start doubting as that could spoil things by causing confusion and uncertainty. Instead, go with this feeling.

Let the momentum pick up and ride the waves with

enthusiasm and excitement. It's okay to be buzzing with joy. Once you believe it is real, the more likely your dream or goal will be brought to fruition because it is picking up on your energetic vibrations through your senses, and everything is working in accordance with what is meant to be.

By this time, you may have found you are already making physical preparations. This is great because it is also a sign that you are sending out to God and the Universe that you trust that it will happen. When you put your trust and energy into an idea, something electric and magical happens. It's almost like a life force is initiated so that everything combines to make it happen. It's a bit like destiny. It's just meant to be.

Preparation is the key to make things happen, and it all starts with mental preparation before the physical can take place. Once this is visible, this is when you can start seeing things come to fruition and then begin seeing things for yourself fall into place. In a way, you expect it, but it's a little more than that. You have started the process of making it happen, and God has taken care of the rest.

Not everything will be plain sailing, there are likely to be times in life when things aren't just handed on a plate to us. Sometimes we have to show that we really want it; occasionally we have to 'get off our laurels' and do something about it. We have to prepare for success and put things into action by giving it a kick-start. I recall someone comparing action to being like the currency of success because it is necessary and you have to take a series of actions in order to make things happen and then the results will follow. What efforts you give out, whether it's from mental or physical work or a combination of both, will be rewarded to you in some way. You could receive an unexpected rebate or someone contacts you out of the blue with an amazing opportunity. You are sowing the seed for your success. By taking action, you are indirectly bridging the gap between your dream and reality. You are putting your plans in motion.

When you prepare for something, you believe that it will happen and are making way for things to come. You are inviting the good into your life. This isn't limited to objects; it could mean inviting good people, events, feelings, and environments.

Don't be afraid of the effort it may take, because after you have prepared, that's when you have made space for the real magic to happen.

Chapter 19

ABUNDANCE

Abundance is a good thing. It creates opportunities to enhance and create. It can transform lives in a positive way and build bridges between the fortunate and not-so-fortunate. This being said, it all depends on how you view abundance.

Your perspective on abundance may have been influenced by others around you when you were growing up. What phrases do you remember hearing? Did you see money as a good thing or as a tool to do bad things? You may have heard phrases like 'money is the root of all evil' or watched soap operas where it appeared that the character with lots of money had all the power and used his or her power to do bad things. There may also have been films where the person with less money was portrayed as the 'good' guy or the one who won the heart of the lady. This was particularly popular in the eighties when the female character nearly always became attracted to the good-looking, 'poor' guy who was often a rebel. Without realising this pattern, it can have an effect on how you view money today, if you let it.

Some people are worried about how they may appear or be judged about having money. This may stem from an interpretation of the Bible. However, if you look closely throughout the Bible, there are plenty of examples

where prosperity is encouraged
and thought of as a good thing.

For instance:
'That person is like a tree
planted by streams of water, which
yields its fruit in season and whose
leaf does not wither – whatever they
do prospers.' (Psalms 1:3. NIV)

and

'The seed will grow well, the
vine will yield its fruit, the ground
will produce its crops, and the
heavens will drop their dew. I will
give all these things as an
inheritance to the remnant of this
people.' (Zechariah 8:12, NIV)

Money in itself has no
emotion or motive. It is
indifferent; it only represents
what you decide. Think for a
moment. How do you view
money? If you view it as a bad
thing, then chances are that is the
reason it may symbolise a

177

struggle to you. There's a saying, 'money comes to money,' which means only people who already have plenty of money are able to receive lots of money. This phrase is often said amongst the not so rich about wealthy people. This is an example of how people can put their own personal viewpoints onto money, thus excusing themselves from the responsibility of managing their money.

However, by choosing to view money as a good thing and as an opportunity to create good in the world, then chances are you will attract more of it.

Once you realise how you have been viewing money, you can decide if you are happy with how you see it or if you wish to make changes to these thought patterns. Yes, you can decide to change your mind about it. Just because you believe something to be true one day, doesn't mean you can't change the way you think about it. Your thoughts and ideas do not have to be forever; they are not set in stone.

If you do decide to change your mind and start thinking about money in a good way, you will find it very liberating. It may even feel like a weight has been lifted off your shoulders. You may also start feeling excited and uplifted when you start thinking of all the things you can do with money, especially when it comes to the 'fun' things you can do. It could be travelling, buying a home, going on a shopping spree, throwing a party, starting a business, or whatever fills you with joy and gets you feeling excited and motivated. After all, money is allowed to be enjoyed. I say 'allowed' because some people feel guilty about spending money. They may fear being judged by others less fortunate or have a belief that you are supposed to only do serious things with money. Money is a tool; it is up to you how you choose to use it. It doesn't have to be all serious or all for fun. As with most things, balance is the key to a happy and healthy life, so use money for necessities. Just don't forget to have fun too.

Of course, money is only part of being abundant. It is also good to have an abundance of love, good health, happiness, time, and even freedom. The freedom to do what you love is a great gift as is having the time to do it. This in itself can enrich your life in more ways than you can imagine. For when your heart is filled with love, it brings joy not only to you but also to those around you.

Shower those you love with these gifts; not all gifts have to be material. Sometimes even showing your appreciation for someone is a gift in itself.

A good way of attracting abundance is to feel abundant. What makes you feel rich? It could be getting your hair done; having a long, relaxing, bubble bath; going out for a meal with loved ones; or even having groceries delivered to you. When you feel like you have plenty, it attracts more to you. It could mean having plenty of food, fun, or even quality time with your friends, family, or by yourself. It's all about how you feel.

Visualising or daydreaming, as I mentioned in Chapter 4, can also help because your subconscious cannot tell the difference between what is real or a dream. It responds the same way for both. That is why when you awake from having a beautiful dream, it puts you in a good mood. Your mind thinks that the event really happened in your reality and this can trigger your emotions to react accordingly. That's why visualisation and meditation can help. They are a shortcut to creating those good feelings before they actually occur. The more you have these feelings, the better your chances are of experiencing them in your everyday life because like attracts like and you get more of what you focus on. Your energy field is a powerful resource and a positive stream of abundance can generate from it if it is used for good and in the right way.

Don't be afraid of feeling abundant. It doesn't have to cost much, and you can receive so much from it. The bonus is that you can share these feelings with others and spread these good feelings of abundance wherever you go. Just like in fairy tales, you are sprinkling fairy dust or magic wherever you go. This way everyone can enjoy feeling abundant.

Chapter 20

CELEBRATE

Celebrating can mean different things to different people. To one person, it can be a reason to pop champagne and have a party with lots of people, and to another, it can be a reason to have a vacation he or she has always dreamt of.

If you are one of those people who seldom takes the time to celebrate because you feel you are too busy and are used to swiftly moving on from one task or deadline to another, this could lead to overwhelm and burnout.

It is important to take the time to appreciate you and all you have accomplished regularly. Not only is this good for your mind and your spirit, it is also good for your health and your overall energy levels. When you have something to celebrate, it triggers those happy feelings in the brain, and you start feeling excited, and life feels worthwhile. Your adrenaline naturally picks up, giving you the energy to be more and do more.

This energy may come from you, but once you tell others of your happy news, it gives them hope, and they also start feeling positive. This ignites energy within themselves, which can bounce over to you and also to other people around them. It's an almost explosive feeling that bursts with positivity and happiness. No matter how other people may be feeling, most can't help but feel joy when people around them are celebrating.

Success attracts success; there are no two ways about it. People always want to know those who are successful, whether it's to learn how to become successful or because they are a little envious and want what they have. This is perfectly natural, and as you grow and accomplish more throughout your life, it is inevitable you will attract more and more people like this.

Don't let that put you off; in fact, take it as a sign of accomplishment. Envy can come from many people around you, even those you would least expect it from, such as a sibling or close friend. Regardless of their intentions, remember, people always want to know the latest success story.

Make an effort to celebrate often, regardless if it is a minor accomplishment or a huge one. In metaphysical terms, the more often you celebrate, the more you will attract things to celebrate. For like attracts like and what you give out you get back, so the more accomplishments or events you have to celebrate, the more reasons you will have to celebrate in the future, which is always a good thing for everyone.

Celebrating the smallest milestone can make all the difference to your overall mood and can give you the momentum to continue even through bleak times. Hold on to these moments of success by taking photos, writing down events, and remembering how these moments made you feel. You may even want to 'anchor' feelings of success (as described in Chapter 2).

You may also find that when you get into the habit of

celebrating your success or that of someone close to you, you have more momentum so you find reasons to celebrate more often.

When you win an award or achieve a goal of some kind, you reach more people, and the more people hear about you, the more opportunities open up for you. This will attract more opportunities for success into your life, and then more people will want to get to know what you are all about, and this will lead to even more opportunities.

Some people may feel a little embarrassed or even a little guilty about this and refrain from shouting so loud in celebration in case they come across as conceited. If this is you; let go of these feelings because they are not serving you. If you keep it to yourself, you are not helping anyone, not even yourself. Don't be afraid of being a success.

You have a right to live a happy, balanced life, and part of that includes being happy and enjoying your life. You have a right to celebrate your achievements and success.

If you find you have a fear of success, there are some tools that can help. Get quiet and try to remember where these memories first stem from. Perhaps it is a childhood memory when you were told not to show anyone something you achieved because a sibling or other children would get jealous and pick on you. Get to the bottom of it and ask yourself how relevant that memory is to you today. EFT, which I mentioned in Chapter 2, is a great tool that can help you release these limiting beliefs by tapping on certain meridian points of your body. I have used this several times, and it has helped me tremendously. If you would like to find out more about this, there are many qualified practitioners on the internet, or you can watch videos to help you practise. If this isn't your thing, counselling or coaching can also help you talk about the reasons behind what is limiting you and holding you back. It is so important to get to the bottom of it and resolve this because once you do, you will feel as though a large weight has been lifted off your shoulders. You will feel much lighter, and above all, you will feel that you have a right to celebrate your success.

Life itself can be a celebration, if you let it. Yes, there will be highs and lows. That is why it is so important to make the most of the highs. Get into the moment and embrace it fully because that is what will help carry you through the lows. Live your life fully and with all your heart and soul by giving it your all.

You deserve to celebrate all that life has to offer. What will you celebrate next?

CONCLUSION

When I was in my late teens or early twenties, my mother and I had a conversation. I was telling her about my dreams of wanting to be a singer/songwriter, the songs I had written, and the steps I was taking to make it happen. She was lying in bed, watching the television, and she was smiling throughout the conversation. Then, just as I was about to depart, she looked at me, smiled, and said, 'You are building castles in the sky.'

I immediately retorted, 'No, I'm not' and left the room, even though I wasn't quite sure what she meant at the time.

She was still smiling and said, 'You'll understand one day' as I left and continued watching the television.

She is no longer with us now, but that conversation stayed with me. I didn't realise it at the time, and however it was intended, she had taught me a valuable lesson.

Later in life, I have learnt that you need to build castles in the sky first before you are able to create or turn them into a reality for all to see. As I mentioned earlier in the book, thoughts really can become things, you need to imagine or dream them up in your head first before you are able to make them visible. Take this book for instance. I had the idea in my mind first, and now it is written in a book for you to read.

In hindsight, if I knew then what I know now, perhaps I would have agreed with her, but we live and we learn; it is all part of being human.

So, let us begin by 'building castles in the sky' and enjoy transforming them from clouds into reality.

SHARE THE LOVE

Have you found this book
helpful?
If so, please tell someone about it
by leaving a review.
You could help make a difference
to someone's life.

BIBLIOGRAPHY

Chapter 19 Abundance

Psalms 1:3, Holy Bible: New International Version.

Zechariah 8:12, Holy Bible: New International Version.

ACKNOWLEDGEMENTS

I would like to thank my family and friends who have supported me in writing this book.

To you, my reader, I thank you for taking the time to read my book, which I wrote especially for you, to inspire and encourage you to build your own castles in the sky.

You are all amazing and a blessing to have in my life.

THANK YOU!

ABOUT THE AUTHOR

Pamela Sommers is the author of bestseller, *Life lessons from a 40 Something...* and founder of SommerSparkle, an award-winning online boutique that provides beautiful jewellery & accessories, which have been showcased in a number of publications, including *British Vogue*.

Her debut book, received a 5-star Award of Excellence from *The International Review of Books*.

Her work has also been featured in *Spotlight* magazine, *Inspired Brides* magazine and her tips for entrepreneurs have been featured in the *HuffPost* blog and *House of Coco* magazine.

Pamela is passionate about inspiring others to make their dreams come true. She loves to listen to music, dance, and enjoys horse- riding. She currently lives in London, England with her fiancé and son.

You can find her online at

pamelasommers.com

facebook.com/PamelaSommersOfficial

instagram.com/pamela.sommers

sommersparkle.com

READ MORE FROM THE AUTHOR...

Life Lessons from a 40 something...
Her bestselling, self-improvement book
is filled with big-hearted advice to
empower and inspire you to go for your
dreams, regardless of your current
circumstances. It is based on her real
life.

Here's what people are saying about
it…

*'An easy read and truly inspirational,
even life changing.'*

*'This book imparts lessons, with each
chapter delivering its own lesson theme,
such as "Don't compare yourself to others,"
etc. Some include how the author came to
learn these lessons, and most include why
they are important.*

*As a therapist, these are all the same lessons
that I strive to teach my clients so that may
live healthy lives that are true to their values
and selves. There is great wisdom in this
book, and I wish I had read it when I was
about fifteen. You will be glad you picked it
up, and hopefully you will share it too.'*

*'Sound advice written in an informal
manner from a personal perspective. There
are things in this book that just reading the
words alone will have a massive impact on a
person. Realising you in yourself are enough
can go a long way. For me, this book is about
trusting who you are, even if you're not*

quite sure who that is. After all, you always change and grow… Easily accessible, not preachy, and very insightful.'

'Big-hearted advice from a wise lady. This is a warm and useful book that I would recommend to anyone from the age of 16 to 40. It covers all the issues that make someone a happy, thriving, successful member of society – from love relationships to being confident in the workplace to how to look great. The author writes clearly in a style that can be understood and applied by any age group, and she gives examples of exercise you can use to implement the ideas she suggests…The new material you do take away will help you live a happier, more fulfilled life.'

'Life Lessons is a book that I wish I would have read years ago. It gives you much-needed wisdom to conquer all the obstacles that you will experience in life, as well as give you sound advice for getting through the highs and lows. This is a book that should be read by teenagers and 20 somethings to avoid any quarter life crisis. As I knock on the door of 40, these are lessons that I still can apply.'

'Although geared toward teenagers and young adults, Life Lessons from a 40 something has all sorts of good advice applicable for all ages, even those of us who are 40 something as well. A pleasant read, full of Ms. Sommers personal experiences and the lessons she learned over the years.'- The International Review of Books

Available from Amazon and other selected book retailers.

NOTES

NOTES

NOTES

NOTES

Printed in Great Britain
by Amazon